Common Core
Standards Practice Workbook

Grade 1

Glenview, Illinois • Boston, Massachusetts
Chandler, Arizona • Upper Saddle River, New Jersey

ALWAYS LEARNING

PEARSON

ISBN-13: 978-0-328-75684-1
ISBN-10:   0-328-75684-9

PEARSON

18   20

Grade 1 Contents

 **Standards Practice**

Operations and Algebraic Thinking . . . . CC 1
Number and Operations in Base Ten . . . . CC 17
Measurement and Data . . . . CC 29
Geometry . . . . CC 37

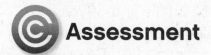 **Assessment**

Practice End-of-Year Assessment . . . . CC 43

About this Workbook

Pearson is pleased to offer this **Common Core Standards Practice Workbook**. In it, you will find pages to help you become good math thinkers and problem-solvers. It includes these pages:

- **Common Core Standards Practice pages.** For each Common Core Standard, you will find two pages of practice exercises. On these pages, you will find different kinds of exercises that are similar to the items expected to be on the end-of-year assessments you will be taking starting in Grade 3. Some of the exercises will have more than one correct answer! Be sure to read each exercise carefully and be on the look-out for exercises that ask you to circle "all that apply" or "all that are correct." They will likely have more than one correct answer.

- **Practice for the Common Core Assessment.** You will find a practice assessment, similar to the Next Generation Assessment that you will be taking. The Practice End-of-Year Assessment has 35 items that are all aligned to the Common Core Standards for Mathematical Content.

Name _____

Common Core Standards Practice

1.OA.A.1 Use addition and subtraction within 20 to solve word problems involving situations of adding to, taking from, putting together, taking apart, and comparing, with unknowns in all positions, e.g., by using objects, drawings, and equations with a symbol for the unknown number to represent the problem.

1. Sara has 5 stuffed animals.
Her sister has 13 stuffed animals.

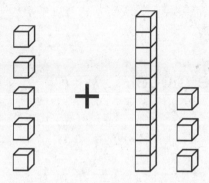

How many stuffed animals   _____
do they have together?   - - - - - - - -
                                _____

· ·

2. Twelve frogs swim in the pond. Eight frogs
jump out of the pond. How many frogs are in
the pond now?

Write a number sentence to match the story.
Use ? for the unknown.

Solve the number sentence you wrote.

_____
- - - - - - - -
_____

3. Fifteen dogs run in the dog park in the morning.
Nine dogs run in the dog park in the afternoon.
How many more dogs run in the dog park in
the morning than in the afternoon?

Draw a model to show the story.

Write a number sentence to match the model.

Solve the number sentence you wrote.

_____

- - - - - - - -

_____

4. Chloe has 8 balloons.
Salma gives her 5 more balloons.
How many balloons does Chloe have now?

Ⓐ 3   Ⓒ 13

Ⓑ 10   Ⓓ 15

Name _____

Common Core Standards Practice

1.OA.A.2 Solve word problems that call for addition of three whole numbers whose sum is less than or equal to 20, e.g., by using objects, drawings, and equations with a symbol for the unknown number to represent the problem.

1. Lia has 8 tiger stickers, 4 turtle
   stickers, and 6 dog stickers.

How many animal stickers does Lia have in all?

_____
- - - - - - - -
_____

....

2. Five children are playing at the park.
   Eight more children join them.
   Later, four more children come.

   Draw a model to show the story.

How many children are   _____
at the park now?   - - - - - - - -
                                _____

3. Maya has 6 apples. Tristan has 7 apples.
Colin has 3 apples.

How many apples do they have altogether?

_____

- - - - - - - -

_____

4. Maria has 7 red marbles, 9 blue marbles,
and 4 white marbles.

Write a number sentence to match the story.
Use ? for the unknown.

Solve the number sentence you wrote.

_____

- - - - - - - -

_____

Name _____

Common Core Standards Practice

1.OA.B.3 Apply properties of operations as strategies to add and subtract.

1. Ava picks 8 ears of corn.
Marta picks 5 ears of corn.

How many ears of corn
do they pick in all?

_____
- - - - - - - - - - -
_____

....

2. David writes $4 + 7 = 11$ another way.
Which shows what David writes?

(A) $4 + 11 = 7$

(B) $11 + 4 = 7$

(C) $4 + 4 = 8$

(D) $7 + 4 = 11$

CC 5

3. Which shows another way to write
5 + 3 + 5 = 13?

    Ⓐ   5 + 5 + 3 = 13

    Ⓑ   5 + 5 + 5 = 13

    Ⓒ   5 + 3 + 3 = 13

    Ⓓ   3 + 3 + 3 = 13

4. Jada sees 12 snails on the sidewalk.
Then 3 snails move into the grass.

How many snails are left on the sidewalk?

_____
- - - - - - - - -
_____

5. Vincent has 14 feathers.
He gives 8 feathers to Josh.
How many feathers does Vincent have left?

Name _____

Common Core Standards Practice

1.OA.B.4 Understand subtraction as an unknown-addend problem.

1. Which addition fact can you
   use to solve $13 - 7$?

   (A) $13 + 6 = 19$

   (B) $7 + 6 = 13$

   (C) $7 + 5 = 12$

   (D) $7 + 13 = 20$

....

2. Ella has 9 buttons.
   She sews some buttons on a pillow.
   She has 2 buttons left.
   She writes this subtraction sentence.

   $9 - \boxed{} = 2$

   How can she write the sentence as an
   addition sentence?

   _____ $+$ $\boxed{}$ $=$ _____

3. There are 14 frogs near a pond.
Then 6 frogs hop away.
Which addition fact helps you find how many
frogs are left?

Ⓐ $14 + 6 = 20$

Ⓑ $6 + 9 = 15$

Ⓒ $6 + 8 = 14$

Ⓓ $6 + 6 = 12$

4. Moshe has 11 pears.
He gives 5 pears to his sister.

Write a subtraction sentence to match the
problem.

_____ – _____ = ☐

Write an addition sentence that Moshe can use.

_____ + ☐ = _____

How many pears does he have now?

Moshe has _____ pears.

Common Core Standards Practice

1.OA.C.5 Relate counting to addition and subtraction (e.g., by counting on 2 to add 2).

1.

Which matches the model?

(A) $6 + 7$

(B) $4 + 5$

(C) $3 + 3$

(D) $3 + 4$

....

2.

Which matches the model?

(A) $10 - 8$

(B) $10 - 2$

(C) $8 - 2$

(D) $8 + 10$

CC 9

3.

Which matches the model?

Ⓐ $6 - 2 - 2 = 2$

Ⓑ $4 + 2 + 2 + 2 = 10$

Ⓒ $4 + 1 + 1 + 1 = 7$

Ⓓ $10 - 2 - 2 - 2 = 4$

4.

Which matches the model?

Ⓐ $8 + 3$

Ⓑ $8 - 3$

Ⓒ $8 - 7$

Ⓓ $7 - 5$

5.

Write an addition sentence that matches the model.

___ ◯ ___ ◯ ___ ◯ ___

Name _____

Common Core Standards Practice

1.OA.C.6 Add and subtract within 20, demonstrating fluency for addition and subtraction within 10. Use strategies such as counting on; making ten (e.g., 8 + 6 = 8 + 2 + 4 = 10 + 4 = 14); decomposing a number leading to a ten (e.g., 13 − 4 = 13 − 3 − 1 = 10 − 1 = 9); using the relationship between addition and subtraction (e.g., knowing that 8 + 4 = 12, one knows 12 − 8 = 4); and creating equivalent but easier or known sums (e.g., adding 6 + 7 by creating the known equivalent 6 + 6 + 1 = 12 + 1 = 13).

I. Raul will add 8 + 7.

Which can help Raul to find the sum?

Ⓐ 7 + 7 + 1   Ⓒ 7 + 8 + 1

Ⓑ 8 + 6 + 1   Ⓓ 6 + 6 + 1

2. Find the sum.

4 + 6 = _____

3. Here is a subtraction problem.

14 − 8 = _____

Which addition sentence can be used to help solve the problem?

Ⓐ 4 + 10 = 14   Ⓒ 6 + 8 = 14

Ⓑ 5 + 9 = 14   Ⓓ 7 + 7 = 14

CC 11

4. Find the difference.

$9 - 3 =$ _____

5. Look at the number line.

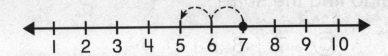

Write a number sentence to match the number line.

_____ ◯ _____ ◯ _____

6. Ama will find the difference.

$16 - 7 = \boxed{}$

Which can help Ama find the difference?

(A) $10 - 6 - 7$

(B) $16 - 6 - 1$

(C) $16 - 8 + 1$

(D) $16 - 7 - 1$

Name _____

Common Core Standards Practice

1.OA.D.7 Understand the meaning of the equal sign, and determine if equations involving addition and subtraction are true or false.

I. Look at the picture below.

Draw triangles to the right of the equal sign to make the sentence true.

Write a number sentence to match the picture.

_____ ◯ _____ ◯ _____

....

2. Circle the number sentences that are true.

$2 + 2 = 4$ $5 - 2 = 4$

$16 + 2 = 17$ $18 - 9 = 9$

....

3. Look at the picture below.

Draw faces to the right of the equal sign to make the sentence true.

Write a number sentence to match the picture.

_____ ◯ _____ ◯ _____

4. Look at the addition sentence below.

Is this sentence true or false? _____

Explain how you know.

. . . .

5. Look at the subtraction sentence below.

Is this sentence true or false? _____

Explain how you know.

Name _____

Common Core Standards Practice

1.OA.D.8 Determine the unknown whole number in an addition or subtraction equation relating three whole numbers.

1. Fill in the missing number to make each sentence true.

$6 +$ _____ $= 7$

_____ $+ 4 = 9$

_____ $+ 1 = 11$

2. Look at the picture below.

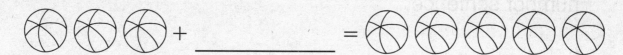

Draw balls to make the sentence true.

Write a number sentence to describe the picture.

3. What number belongs in the box below?

$6 + \boxed{} = 12$

Ⓐ 0   Ⓑ 3   Ⓒ 6   Ⓓ 12

CC 15

4. Fill in the missing number to make each sentence true.

$$8 + \underline{\hspace{2cm}} = 9$$

$$\underline{\hspace{2cm}} + 5 = 10$$

$$6 + \underline{\hspace{2cm}} = 12$$

5. Find the sum. Draw a model to match the number sentence.

$$4 + 6 = \underline{\hspace{2cm}}$$

6. What number belongs in the box?

$$\boxed{} - 8 = 6$$

Ⓐ 6   Ⓒ 10

Ⓑ 8   Ⓓ 14

Name _____

Common Core Standards Practice

1.NBT.A.1 Count to 120, starting at any number less than 120. In this range, read and write numerals and represent a number of objects with a written numeral.

1. What comes next? Write the next three numbers.

57, 58, 59, _____, _____, _____

---

2. How many cubes are there? Write the number.

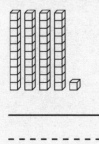

_____
- - - - - - - -
_____

---

3. Julie has 34 counters. Show 34 counters.

4. What number comes next? Write the next three numbers.

81, 82, 83, _____, _____, _____

5. Bill has 26 squares. Show 26 squares.

6. How many stars are there? Count the stars. Write the number.

_____

- - - - - - - -

_____

Name _____

Common Core Standards Practice

1.NBT.B.2 Understand that the two digits of a two-digit number represent amounts of tens and ones. Understand the following as special cases: 10 can be thought of as a bundle of ten ones—called a "ten."; The numbers from 11 to 19 are composed of a ten and one, two, three, four, five, six, seven, eight, or nine ones; The <u>numbers</u> 10, 20, 30, 40, 50, 60, 70, 80, 90 refer to one, two, three, four, five, six, seven, eight, or nine tens (and 0 ones).

1. Laura writes the number 35.

How many tens?

_____
- - - - - - - -
_____

How many ones?

_____
- - - - - - - -
_____

2. What is the value of the digit 1 in this number?

21

Ⓐ 1   Ⓑ 2   Ⓒ 10   Ⓓ 20

3. Priya writes the number 46.

How many tens?

_____
- - - - - - - -
_____

How many ones?

_____
- - - - - - - -

4. Andrew writes the number 19.

How many tens?

_____

- - - - - - - - -

_____

How many ones?

_____

- - - - - - - - -

_____

....

5. What is the value of the digit 9 in this number?

92

Ⓐ   9

Ⓑ   20

Ⓒ   90

Ⓓ   92

....

6. A number has a 7 in the tens place.
A number has a 2 in the ones place.
What is the number?

_____

- - - - - - - - -

_____

CC 20

Name _____

Common Core Standards Practice

1.NBT.B.3 Compare two two-digit numbers based on meanings of the tens and ones digits, recording the results of comparisons with the symbols >, =, and <.

1. Insert < , > , or = between the numbers.

23 _____ 50

35 _____ 25

54 _____ 53

99 _____ 99

....

2. Lilly compared 24 and 16

24 $\boxed{<}$ 16

Is Lilly correct?

Yes   No

How do you know?

3. Oscar has three number cards.

4	2	8

Write the greatest two-digit
number Oscar can make.

_ _ _ _ _ _ _ _ _ _ _ _ _ _ _ _

Write the least two-digit
number Oscar can make.

_ _ _ _ _ _ _ _ _ _ _ _ _ _ _ _

Use <, >, or = to compare the two numbers.

4. Nick compared two numbers.

86 | < | 83

Is Nick correct?

Yes   No

How do you know?

Name _____

Common Core Standards Practice

1.NBT.C.4 Add within 100, including adding a two-digit number and a one-digit number, and adding a two-digit number and a multiple of 10, using concrete models or drawings and strategies based on place value, properties of operations, and/or the relationship between addition and subtraction; relate the strategy to a written method and explain the reasoning used. Understand that in adding two-digit numbers, one adds tens and tens, ones and ones; and sometimes it is necessary to compose a ten.

I. Which number belongs in the box?

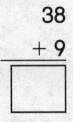

$$\begin{array}{r} 38 \\ +\ 9 \\ \hline \boxed{} \end{array}$$

Ⓐ 29 Ⓒ 47

Ⓑ 37 Ⓓ 108

---

2. Maya will add these two numbers.

Tens	Ones
3	I
+	7

Why does she add 7 and I?

Why doesn't she add 3 and 7?

3. Add:

$$63$$
$$+ \, 10$$
_____

4. What number belongs in the box?

$$87$$
$$+ \, 4$$

(A) 20   (C) 111

(B) 91   (D) 174

5. Jamie adds these two numbers

$$58$$
$$+ \, 20$$

Why does she add 5 and 2?

Why doesn't she add 8 and 2?

Name _____

Common Core Standards Practice

1.NBT.C.5 Given a two-digit number, mentally find 10 more or 10 less than the number, without having to count; explain the reasoning used.

1. What number is 10 more than 44?

_____

- - - - - - - -

_____

2. What number is 10 less than 73?

_____

- - - - - - - -

_____

Explain your answer using words or drawings.

3. What number is 10 less than 96?

_____

- - - - - - - -

_____

Explain your answer using words or drawings.

4. What number is 10 more than 49?

_____

- - - - - - - -

_____

Name _____

Common Core Standards Practice

1.NBT.C.6 Subtract multiples of 10 in the range 10–90 from multiples of 10 in the range 10–90 (positive or zero differences), using concrete models or drawings and strategies based on place value, properties of operations, and/or the relationship between addition and subtraction; relate the strategy to a written method and explain the reasoning used.

1.

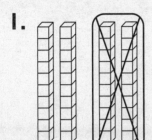

Write a number sentence that matches the model.

2. Solve.

$80 - 10 =$ _____

Draw or write to explain your answer.

3. Which model matches this subtraction sentence?

$$70 - 40 = 30$$

 Ⓐ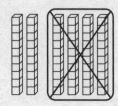

Ⓒ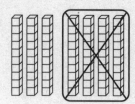

Ⓑ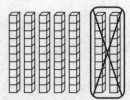

Ⓓ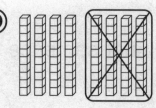

- -

4. Abby has 30 cards. Sam has 20 cards. How many more cards does Abby have?

Draw or write to explain your answer.

CC 28

Name _____

Common Core Standards Practice

1.MD.A.1 Order three objects by length; compare the lengths of two objects indirectly by using a third object.

1. Look at the pencils.

Put a circle around the shortest pencil.

Put an X on the longest pencil.

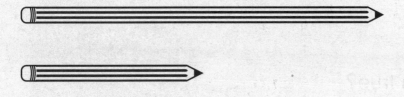

2. Which is longer? Circle it.

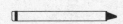

Write **shorter** or **longer** to complete the sentence.

The crayon is _____ than the feather.

3. Look at the objects.

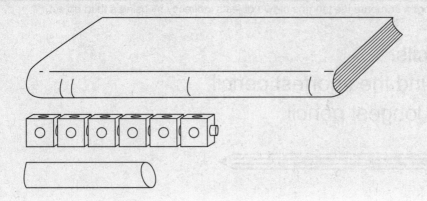

Which sentence is true?

Ⓐ The book is shorter than the chalk.

Ⓑ The chalk is longer than the cube train.

Ⓒ The chalk is shorter than the book.

Ⓓ The book is shorter than the cube train.

4. Draw a thick line and a thin line. Make the thick line longer.

Name _____

Common Core Standards Practice

1.MD.A.2 Express the length of an object as a whole number of length units, by laying multiples copies of a shorter object (the length unit) end to end; understand that the length measurement of an object is the number of same-size length units that span it with no gaps or overlaps. *Limit to contexts where the object being measured is spanned by a whole number of length units with no gaps or overlaps.*

I. Evan has a piece of string.

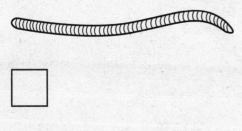

☐

How many squares long is Evan's string?

_____

- - - - - - - - - - -

_____

....

2. How many squares long is the paintbrush?

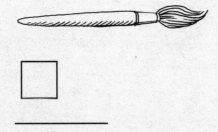

☐

_____

- - - - - - - - - - -

_____

Explain how you measured.

3. How many squares long is the key?

□

_____
- - - - - - - -
_____

---

4. How many squares long is the crayon?

□

_____
- - - - - - - -
_____

Explain how you measured.

Name _____

Common Core Standards Practice

1.MD.B.3 Tell and write time in hours and half-hours using analog and digital clocks.

I. What time does the clock show?

(A) 4:00

(B) 4:30

(C) 5:00

(D) 5:30

- -

2. Mary has soccer practice at four-thirty. Write this time in the clock below.

3. What time does the clock show? Write the time below.

____ : ____

....

4. What time does the clock show?

Ⓐ seven-thirty

Ⓑ seven o'clock

Ⓒ eight-thirty

Ⓓ eight o'clock

Name _____

Common Core Standards Practice

1.MD.C.4 Organize, represent, and interpret data with up to three categories; ask and answer questions about the total number of data points, how many in each category, and how many more or less are in one category than in another.

Brad asks his friends to name their favorite color.

Five friends say blue.
Six friends say red.
Four friends say green.

I. Complete the tally chart to show the results.

Favorite Colors

Blue	
Red	
Green	

2. Use the tally chart to make a bar graph.

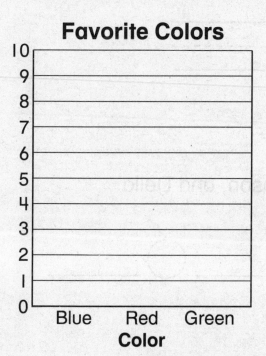

Favorite Colors

Use the picture graph to answer the questions.

Books Read

Emily	▱▱▱▱
Mason	▱▱▱▱▱▱▱
Delia	▱▱▱▱▱▱▱▱

▱ = 1 book.

3. How many books did
   Mason read?   _____
                                  _____

4. How many more books did Delia read than Emily?
   Write a number sentence to solve.

   _____ ◯ _____ ◯ _____

                                  _____
   Solve the number sentence.   _____

5. How many books did Emily, Mason, and Delia
   read altogether?

   _____ ◯ _____ ◯ _____ ◯ _____

Name _____

Common Core Standards Practice

1.G.A.1 Distinguish between defining attributes (e.g., triangles are closed and three-sided) versus non-defining attributes (e.g., color, orientation, overall size); build and draw shapes to possess defining attributes.

1. Skylar draws a square.

What makes it a square?

Ⓐ It has 4 equal sides.

Ⓑ It is big.

Ⓒ It is white.

Ⓓ It is right side up.

2. Draw a shape that has 3 sides and 3 corners.

3. Carter draws a rectangle.

What is true about all rectangles?

Ⓐ They have 3 sides.

Ⓑ They have 4 corners.

Ⓒ They are small.

Ⓓ They are white.

....

4. Draw a shape with 5 sides.

Name _____

Common Core Standards Practice

1.G.A.2 Compose two-dimensional shapes (rectangles, squares, trapezoids, triangles, half-circles, and quarter-circles) or three-dimensional shapes (cubes, right rectangular prisms, right circular cones, and right circular cylinders) to create a composite shape, and compose new shapes from the composite shape.

I. Aidan has these 2 shapes.

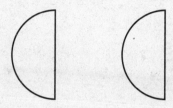

Circle the shape he can make if he puts
the 2 shapes together.

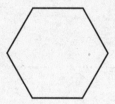 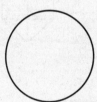

2. Combine these 2 shapes to
make a new shape.
Draw the new shape.

3. Brynn has these 2 shapes.

Circle the shape she can make if she puts
the 2 shapes together.

---

4. Look at the shape.

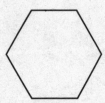

Circle the 2 shapes that can be used to make
the shape above.

         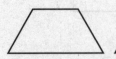 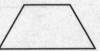

Name _____

Common Core Standards Practice

1.G.A.3 Partition circles and rectangles into two and four equal shares, describe the shares using the words *halves*, *fourths*, and *quarters*, and use the phrases *half of*, *fourth of*, and *quarter of*. Describe the whole as two of, or four of the shares. Understand for these examples that decomposing into more equal shares creates smaller shares.

1. Draw a line to make two equal parts.

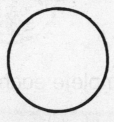

Circle the name of one of the parts.

half   fourth   quarter

2. Look at the square.

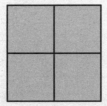

Is the square divided into halves, thirds, or fourths? Tell how you know.

3. Circle the pizza with bigger pieces.

Austin's pizza   Lilly's pizza

Use one of these words to complete each sentence.

halves   thirds   fourths

Austin's pizza is cut into _____.

Lilly's pizza is cut into _____.

4. Draw lines to divide the rectangle into fourths.

Practice End-of-Year Assessment

Name _____

1. Martin has 14 marbles.
His brother gives him 5 more marbles.
How many marbles does he have now?

Write a number sentence. Use ? for the unknown.

Solve the number sentence you wrote. _ _ _ _ _ _ _ _

2. How many strawberries are there?
Write the number.

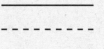

_ _ _ _ _ _ _ _

3. Which sentence is true?

Ⓐ 16 − 8 = 8   Ⓒ 14 − 7 = 5

Ⓑ 13 − 5 = 7   Ⓓ 17 − 9 = 9

CC 43

4. Find the sum.

$5 + 6 + 9$

_____
- - - - - - - - -
_____

5. Simon walks 11 blocks to school.
Leo walks 4 blocks to school.
How many more blocks
does Simon walk than Leo?

Ⓐ 5

Ⓑ 6

Ⓒ 7

Ⓓ 8

6. Circle the longest straw.
Cross out the shortest straw.

7. Write an addition sentence to help you solve the subtraction sentence.

$14 - 8 = $ _____

_____ ◯ _____ ◯

- - - - - - -

Solve the subtraction sentence. _____

_____

8. Draw a line to make 2 equal parts.

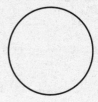

Circle the name of one of the parts.

half   fourth   quarter

9. What number makes the sentence true?

$14 - \boxed{} = 5$

Ⓐ 7   Ⓒ 9

Ⓑ 8   Ⓓ 10

10. Aiden has these 2 shapes.

Circle the shape he can make
if he puts the 2 shapes together.

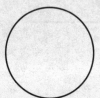 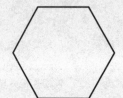

11. Draw a line to make 4 equal parts.

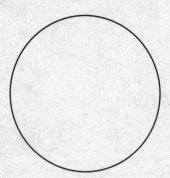

12. Which addition sentence helps you find the
missing number?

$12 - \boxed{} = 7$

(A) $7 + 4 = 11$ (C) $7 + 3 = 10$

(B) $7 + 5 = 12$ (D) $6 + 6 = 12$

13. Write a number sentence that matches the model.

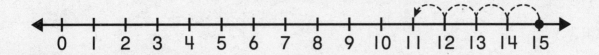

_____ ◯ _____ ◯ _____

14. Write $<$, $>$, or $=$ to make the sentence true.

32 ◯ 41

15. Circle the addition sentences that are true.
Cross out the sentences that are false.

9 + 8 = 17   8 + 4 = 13

12 + 5 = 19   11 + 4 = 15

16. What is the value of the digit 4 in this number?

74

....

17. Amelia has 17 crayons.
She leaves 8 of them at her grandma's house.
How many crayons does she have now?

Write a number sentence
to solve the problem.   _____ ◯ _____ ◯ _____

Solve the number sentence.   _____

....

18. Use paper clips to measure the width
of a book in your classroom.
How many paper clips wide
is the book?

_____

19. George and Pam pick strawberries at the farm.
George picks 8 strawberries and Pam picks 9.
How many strawberries do they pick?

Write a number sentence to match the problem.

_____ ◯ _____ ◯ _____

_____

Solve the number sentence.   _____

20. What is the missing number?   _____

$12 + \boxed{} = 18$ _____

21. Mathias asks his friends which vegetable they
like best.
His results are in the tally chart.

Favorite Vegetable

Corn	ⅢⅡ I
Beans	ⅢⅡ III
Broccoli	IIII

Make a picture graph to display the
Mathias' results.

Favorite Vegetable

Corn	
Beans	
Broccoli	

☺ = I friend.

22. What is the sum?

$$7$$
$$+\ 9$$

---

23. Which number makes the sentence true?

$$6 + \boxed{} = 15$$

Ⓐ 7

Ⓑ 8

Ⓒ 9

Ⓓ 10

---

24. Write the time shown on the clock.

———:———

25. Sarah subtracts $14 - 8$.
This shows how she subtracts.
$$14 - 4 = 10$$
$$10 - 4 = 6$$

Which strategy does she use?

Ⓐ count on

Ⓑ make a ten

Ⓒ count back

Ⓓ use addition to subtract

26. Help Aubrey add $7 + 9$.
Show two ways to add these numbers.

One way	Another way

27. What number is 10 less than 27?

_____

- - - - - - - -

_____

28. Write $<$, $>$, or $=$ to compare.

64 $\bigcirc$ 64

29. Anna adds 5 and 5 to get 10. Tell which strategy she uses.

30. Draw a figure with 4 sides.

31. Daisy has 9 pencils.
Jaden has 8 pencils.
How many pencils do they have together?

Write a number sentence to match the story.

_____ ◯ _____ ◯ _____

Solve the number sentence.

_____

- - - - - - - -

_____

32. Grace draws 3 cats.
She draws 5 dogs.
She draws 6 hamsters.
How many animals does she
draw in all?

Write a number sentence
to match the story.

_____ ◯ _____ ◯ _____ ◯ _____

Solve the number sentence.

_____

- - - - - - - -

_____

CC 53

33. Anthony has 54 crayons.
Write 54 as tens and ones.

_____ tens _____ ones

34. Find the difference.

$60 - 30$

_____
- - - - - - -
_____

35. Natalie adds $7 + 8$.
Look at what she does.
$7 + 7 = 14$
$14 + 1 = 15$
Which strategy does she use?

Ⓐ doubles plus 1   Ⓒ count on

Ⓑ make a ten   Ⓓ doubles